How to Direct a Business

7 Skills You Must Develop to Succeed

Table of Contents

Introduction

Thank you and congratulations for purchasing *"How to Direct a Business:* 7 Skills You Must Develop to Succeed".

This book was designed to help you succeed in your business, regardless of where you are in the present. Whether you are brand new to the world of business, or if you have been in it for a while but are looking to improve your skills, this book will help ensure that you learn the necessary steps to mastering the process.

Running a business is as much about mindset as it is about action, which you will learn about throughout this book. You will be given actionable skills that you can understand and work on immediately, regardless of any existing or non-existing circumstances that you may be facing. That means that you are not required to have any specific amount of finances, employees, customers, or otherwise to begin developing and utilizing these skills immediately. Instead, these skills will work towards moving you toward success no matter where you are currently.

If you are ready to discover what it takes to run a business and succeed, this book will teach you exactly what is required. So, please read on, and enjoy!

Chapter 1: Self-Discipline

The first and most important step when it comes to running a business is self-discipline. Nothing will serve you greater than a strong sense of self-discipline. This skill is important for the business itself, and it is also important for being a leader. Naturally, if you are an entrepreneur, you are also a leader. Whether you already possess the qualities of a strong leader or not, you have assumed the leadership role in your company. Therefore, you need to ensure that you are regularly working toward developing your skills to make yourself into a strong leader.

Self-discipline is a common trait shared by all people who have experienced any level of success. The more disciplined a person is, the greater their success will be. Discipline is the skill you need that will take you out of the "thinking" state and put you into the "action" state. Many people don't make this transition because they find comfort in thinking. Thinking about something, in their mind, means that they meant to do it. Because they had good intentions, they assume they did a good job. Of course, this is completely false. However, many people use this strange justification to keep themselves in the thinking state and prevent themselves from ever having to put forth the effort to enter the action state. If you want to be successful, though, you need to jump into action. This is where having a strong sense of self-discipline will help you. You will be able to recognize that simply thinking is not enough and that you need to take action. Then, you will be able to take the necessary action to achieve results.

There are many ways that your discipline will show up in and serve your business. From helping you generate goals to ensuring that you actively work toward them, discipline is the glue that holds it all together. This is the skill that keeps you rising in the morning even though you don't technically have to, keeps you showing up and working even though there isn't anyone technically making sure you do, and ensures that you take productive action rather than wasting time on mindless tasks even though there isn't technically anyone you are trying to impress. Do you see how most people rely on technicalities to get themselves out of taking disciplined and focused action?

This can't be you.

If you want to run a business, you absolutely must focus on developing your sense of self-discipline. When you focus and apply yourself to creating this one specific skill, every other skill you are going to learn in this book and anywhere else in life becomes infinitely more usable. That is because you will have the self-discipline required to read it and do it, not simply read about it and pretend to do it. Are you still noticing all of the differences between self-disciplined and not disciplined? I hope so.

To truly ensure that you understand the difference between a lack of discipline and a great sense of discipline, let's look at two different examples. In the first one, we are going to follow George as he goes about his morning routine with the money coaching he does from his computer at home. Then, we will follow William as he goes about his morning routine with the financial advising he does from his computer at home. Notice the differences as you read.

George opens his eyes to the sound of his alarm clock going off at 6 AM. He rubs his eyes, turns the alarm off, and rolls over. "Who is going to be angry if I don't awake? I don't have any appointments until the afternoon, anyway." He says as he goes back to sleep. Several hours later, he wakes up at noon. Shocked, he jumps out of bed and runs for the shower, trying to get himself looking presentable for his Skype interview at 1 PM. A few minutes later he emerges from the shower and runs into the kitchen to grab a coffee and some food. Then, he chows it back while he opens his laptop and turns it on. He prepares the programs for his meeting, then notices he only has 2 minutes left before it starts. Without enough time to brush his teeth, he looks in his webcam to pick away leftover pieces of food and washes them away with a sip of coffee. By the time his programs are running, it is a few minutes past one, and he calls his client, starting the consultation with an apology for being late.

William opens his eyes at 5:45 AM with a few minutes to spare before his alarm clock went off at 6 AM. He grew so used to waking up early that he often found himself waking up on his own, always a few minutes before the alarm clock would go off. He used this time to relax and think about what he was looking forward to that day. At 5:59 AM he would turn the alarm off to avoid it from waking up his spouse, then he would climb out of bed. First, he would go to the washroom. Then, he would make some coffee and relax with it as he read the morning paper. Once he was done, he would prepare himself and his spouse a nice breakfast to share when she woke up. Then, he would get in the shower and prepare himself for the day. He always dressed up nicely and kept himself well-groomed, despite working from home. He knew that no matter where he was stationed, his clients would see him on the webcam and would not want to see him looking lazy and unkempt. An hour before his first meeting, William checks his calendar. He ensures he is aware of all of the meetings he has going on this day, often noting that he was booked full with consultations and calls. He would schedule out his breaks, plan his day in advance, and then ensure that everything was well prepared and he was briefed on his first client before the call started. He always showed up early to calls so that he was all ready to greet his clients when they showed up on the call. This is how he showed them he cared and that he was genuinely concerned about giving them the highest quality of his services, every time.

In these two very different descriptions, you can clearly see the negative traits that come when you aren't self-disciplined and the positive traits that come when you are. George, who lacked self-disciplined, used technicalities to skate by. Instead of running his company like a business, he was running it like a get-rich-quick scheme with very little attention or consideration. He showed no concern for his client, which is likely why he didn't have many appointments set for the day. Because of his lack of self-discipline, he did himself, his business, and his client a disservice by showing up late for his appointment. He was also not briefed on his client, meaning he had to spend some of the client's valuable time recalling what the call was about in the first place and the client's unique circumstances. It is likely due to his lack of professionalism as a result of his lack of discipline that leads to George not booking many clients. After an experience like this, his client would likely consider him to be unprofessional and would either ask for a refund or refrain from going back, or both. He would also likely tell his friends to avoid George, thus further damaging his ability to book future clients. Because George was incapable of using the type of discipline that is necessary to run a business, his business is not thriving.

William's experience in business is clearly very different from George's. Although they are both in a similar field with a similar business model, William clearly has far more self-discipline when it comes to running his company. Although he could technically sleep in, he always rises early. In fact, he rises early enough that he even gets a few extra minutes before his alarm clock goes off. He also has enough time to spend relaxing, enjoying a healthy breakfast with his spouse, and grooming himself properly before he began his appointment with his client. He also had plenty of time to plan his day, brief himself on his clients, and prepare for his meetings. Because of his self-discipline, William was capable of giving his client a phenomenal experience. This professionalism and productivity are likely how he can book so many clients and run a thriving business, despite not having a boss and team full of employees to help him run his company. Even though he doesn't have anyone standing over him telling him what to do, he is fully capable of getting his work done.

This is what it means to be self-disciplined: you do not need someone telling you what to do. You take the time to recognize what needs to be done, and you do it. This increases your productivity, your professionalism, your customer rating, and ultimately your overall success.

So, how do you get started with being self-disciplined? Naturally, it is much easier to get off on "technicalities." So, being self-disciplined means that you must acquire a certain level of motivation to get yourself going and change your existing habits. Luckily for you, there are only four steps that you need to follow to begin practicing self-discipline and let it help you thrive in your business. Here they are:

- Have a purpose. Most people can be motivated when they are using the right material to motivate them. The key here is to use material that motivates you. It should not be a generic "purpose" that you borrowed from someone online or someone who told you what your purpose should be. Instead, it should be something that drives you. Maybe you want to retire young and have a team full of employees to run your business for you so you can generate residual income. Or, maybe you want to work enough so that your partner can leave their job. Maybe you want to save for a house and afford the lifestyle you want or invest in your children's future, or maybe you have always wanted to be a part of a certain societal club that costs a significant amount of money to cover the membership fee every year. Maybe you always wanted to swim around in a pool of money, so you are working to make enough money that you can comfortably do that. Or maybe your purpose is more to the effect of helping people or donating to charity. It doesn't matter what your purpose is or how superficial it may seem to others.

As long as your purpose makes you eager to work and grow your company, it is plenty good enough.

- Create a plan. It is not enough to have a purpose, but you also need to have a plan for how you want to get there. This is where many people hire business coaches. But, you don't necessarily need to. Instead, you simply need to know what is required for you to get to your purpose. For example, say your purpose is to own a certain house and live a certain lifestyle. Then, your plan would be to build a company that will earn you the annual salary required to live that lifestyle. Build your plan backward, working from your desired salary to what is required for you to earn that salary, and then what is required for you to meet those requirements. Continue working backward until you have a clear idea of what you need to do on a daily, weekly, monthly, and yearly basis. Then, ensure that you revisit that plan on a consistent basis to adjust your course to reflect reality since reality is often different from what we have actually planned.

- Reward yourself. The best companies and bosses often give their employees rewards. Becoming an employee of the month, getting financial bonuses for hitting certain sales goals, and even getting pizza parties for hitting certain goals have all been used as methods for rewarding employees in many major corporations. You should use this as a system to help encourage you to work toward your business goals! When you are planning, identify certain milestones. Then, when you hit these milestones, have pre-planned rewards that you earn at those milestones. Since you are your own boss, you can choose rewards that are motivational and enjoyable for you. For example, a mini-shopping spree, a special dinner at your favorite restaurant, a trip to your favorite place or any other number of enjoyable rewards that are unique to your desires can be used to motivate you. They also encourage you to feel good about your work and to keep moving forward!

- Have trust. It is absolutely imperative that you trust in yourself, your purpose, and your plan. As long as you have invested adequate energy and attention into building both of them, and they are viable, you should feel confident in placing your trust in them. Know that you have the power to move forward and that you are capable of achieving anything you set out to achieve. Know that your plan has been built with that in mind, and work on it with complete faith in its ability to get you where you want to go. When it is time for your check-in, look at areas where your plan served you and areas where it could have been stronger. Then, adjust your plan and entrust it fully again until your next check-in. Never doubt your plan or your purpose, especially if you are confident that you gave your best attention to building them. Work as faithfully on these as you would on an itinerary a boss would give you in your place of business if you were someone's employee.

Invest in your self-discipline on a daily basis so that you can stop squandering your business away on technicalities and start embracing a strong, can-do attitude that actually takes you forward toward your entrepreneurial goals. If you take it one day at a time and focus on taking the most productive action you can each day, while consistently working toward the items outlined on your plan, then you will find yourself running a powerful business that helps you achieve every goal you have ever set out for both your business and yourself.

Chapter 2: Money Management

Major companies and corporations have the added benefits of an entire team dedicated to the financial aspects of their company. These people are responsible for ensuring that said company's budgets are created and followed, that their taxes are filed appropriately, and that all other financial elements of the business are addressed adequately. Because they are trained on this knowledge, they are highly efficient with it, and so the company thrives.

Entrepreneurs don't often have that benefit. While you should likely have an accountant to help give you advice, you are solely responsible for the management of your company's finances. For this reason, it is imperative that you have good money management skills.

Regardless of how much money you have in your company right now, how much it has made, how much it has lost, or any other considerations about your company's finances, you should start building your money management skills immediately. Knowing how to manage your money will prevent you from wasting any money you make, ensure that you are always in the green, and keep you from having any major financial failures in your company. Every strong company should always be operating in the green, or adequately working towards it if they are in debt (such as if you started on a business loan). Here are some tips to help you manage your money better:

Budget

The first and most important step with any company is to budget. When you are creating your budget, you want to take a look at the amount of money your company is making versus the amount of money it is paying out. If you already have an existing company and have not been doing this, take a moment to review what your credit (outgoing) versus debit (incoming) has been in your company for the past three months, or as long as you can. Notice where money is going to, if any is being wasted, and most importantly, if you are profitable or not.

Building your budget should start by identifying two numbers: how much you need, and how much you make. Tally up all of the outgoing expenses you have in your business. This includes everything, including but not limited to: service fees, marketing, rent, insurance, payroll (your earnable income), taxes, and anything else you are currently paying for out of your company money. Then, you want to tally up how much you are making from your business. This would include anything you have invested in with your company, any money your clients pay you, and any other ways you have made money. Now, if your spending value is higher than your earning value, you need to adjust your budget to reduce your spending fees as much as possible. You also know that you need to make an actionable plan to earn more money in your business.

Once you have completed a budget based on existing information, make a budget based on future information. Take the average earned value from the previous months, if available, and use this as your projected income. If you know that you are getting extra money, include this in the value for those months. Then, pay attention to your spending as well. Make a plan so that you know where money is going, when it needs to get there, and how you are going to pay for it.

It is imperative that this budget includes absolutely every incoming and outgoing expense incurred by your business.

Additionally, you need to ensure that you actually stay on track with this budget. When the time comes each month, ensure that every single bill on the "spending" side is paid. Anything that may be left over, have a set plan for what you will do with it. For example, perhaps you will put it in an investment account and let it grow for your business. Or, maybe you will pay it out to yourself as a bonus. No matter how you are going to do it, have a plan for this money in advance so that it doesn't get wasted. You should know where every single dollar is going in your company, and where every single dollar is coming from. If anything changes along the course of the month, always reflect it in your budget. This is the first step in effective money management.

Pay Yourself a Set Amount

Many entrepreneurs think that all money that is paid to them by clients is automatically income. This is actually not true, and this stems from an "employee" perspective rather than a "CEO" perspective. Keeping all of the money you make from your clients means that you are going to be cutting into your own income to pay for the bills associated with your company. Not only does it get confusing, but it also blurs the lines between yourself and your company. If you want to run a business, run your business like a business. Have a distinct and outlined budget for your company and pay yourself a set amount. If you can afford to give yourself a raise or pay out bonuses to yourself under certain circumstances, by all means you can do so. However, have a set amount that you are going to pay yourself from the income you are earning. This way, you can account for your own income as an expense through your business. Then, if you want, you can always set a personal budget for yourself afterward.

CEOs of major corporations would never put all of the money their company makes into their own account. Even if you are running a sole proprietorship, you should refrain from doing this. Keeping your income distinct means that you can budget for it in your company budget. Developing healthy money management skills like this early on will make it significantly easier when it comes time to grow your business, which, if you follow these steps, you inevitably will!

Invest

Investing your money in the right places is valuable. Many companies choose to invest money into actual funds to allow their money to grow. This is great, and you can communicate with your account or a financial advisor if you want to do this with your own company. However, there is another type of investing that you need to consider when it comes to running your business and managing your finances. That is, you need to focus on business growth. Investing in what your company needs to grow is important to expand your company to the level you want to get it to. Even if you have already reached your initial goals for expansion, you should set new goals and continue investing to reach said new goals. Here are some things you need to be investing in for your business:

- Insurance. Every business should be insured. Insuring your business means that you will not be held liable in many different situations, often unique to your individual business model and industry. It also means that if you ever face something such as theft, fire, or some form of damage, your equipment is insured and you can revive your business without any personal expenses incurred. Insurance doesn't only protect you, but it protects your customers, and potentially your building managers and landlord if you rent space. In fact, many landlords will require you to have your business insured if you are going to rent space. Investing in insurance is an important step when it comes to running your business as it protects your assets which is a no-brainer!

- Marketing. Marketing is how you access your customers and increase your sales volumes. When you are running a business, you need to invest in marketing. This investment should include everything you use for marketing, such as advertisements, paid posts, paid influencers, free services/products rendered in exchange for reviews or for giveaways, and anything else to do with promotional events in your company. You should always be investing in your marketing to ensure that you are expanding. You should also pay attention to how your marketing efforts are paying off so that you can invest more in successful ventures and stray away from those that are wasting your budget.

- Outsourcing. Although you may not need to do this immediately, almost every business, even a one-man-show, will need to outsource stuff over time. When you get to that point, always invest in outsourcing. Whether you are hiring a web designer to create your website, an assistant to help you stay on track, or an accountant to help you get your finances in order, you are going to have to make investments. Major corporations have many employees because their employees specialize in different fields, making the corporation run. They know they cannot do everything themselves, so they hire people to do things for them. Although you may not be able to hire a team full of specialized employees, you can still outsource various parts of your business to help offload some of the work and allow you to focus on what you are good at. Since this frees up some of your time so you can be more productive, and allows you to achieve better results along, it is worth the investment.

- Yourself. In an entrepreneurial setting, you are an asset to your business. Especially if you run something smaller, such as a sole proprietorship, you are the star of the show. Investing in yourself means that you can offer better products and services, so it is entirely worth it. The more you know, the more you can give to your company and the bigger it will grow. Invest in yourself by investing in your education. Take courses and attend seminars to learn as much as you can so that you can achieve great success with your company.

- Your Products and Services. The products and services you are offering are always worth the investment. Never cheap out when you are creating your products or services. Get the best manufacturers you can afford, use the best platforms for service-hosting that you can afford, and ensure that all of your content is high quality. The better quality your products and services are, the more appealing it will be to your clients. When they love it, they will refer you to other people, and then your business will grow. Since this is the main attraction for your clients, you absolutely must invest in it.

Save

Of course, it's important to save money as an individual. But, it's also important to save money as a business, too. Business can be volatile, and you are not always going to make the same amount every month. Some months you may have wild success and others you may struggle to get by. Setting up the intention to save money every month, no matter how good or bad the month has been, means that in the months where you are hitting a horrible rut your finances won't be in shambles. You can call on that savings fund to help you pay for your bills until your earning value comes back up. Always save money for your business so that you don't have to invest personal funds in the bills if things aren't going particularly well for a month or two.

Get Professional Help

Remember, corporations have financial advisors because these people are professionally trained to deal with money. You may not be able to afford an entire financial team, but that doesn't mean you shouldn't invest in a high-quality accountant. Accountants are an incredible asset when it comes to running your own business. They know the world of company finances very well. Therefore, they can give you the best advice to get you moving forward and to create financial stability in your company. They will help you budget, invest your money in the right things, and ensure that your taxes are filed properly each year. If you are going to outsource anything, make your first outsourced gig one for an accountant. Getting professional help can make a world of difference in your company's financial well-being.

Chapter 3: Stress Management

A leader is not nearly as valuable if he or she is too stressed out to lead! If you want to have success with your company, you need to work on your stress management skills. A stress-free leader is more capable of leading from a place of clarity and focus. They have greater resilience, confidence, and mental strength to overcome the challenges that are often presented in a business setting. By learning to manage your own stress, you can maximize your success and productivity as a leader, which is vital whether you are running a business entirely on your own or if you are running a business complete with employees and associates.

Managing stress effectively to be a strong leader means that you need to manage stress both in your business life and in your personal life. Whether we intend to or not, the stress we incur outside of the workplace often follows us into our work life. Even when we try and tune out of it, we are simply not capable of relieving ourselves of all of the physical and mental symptoms that come along with being stressed out. So, it is imperative that you focus these stress-management techniques on all aspects of your life to maximize your success as a leader.

The first thing you need to realize is that you are absolutely not going to be able to foster a completely stress-free life and environment when you run a business. This may sound redundant to this entire skill, but it's actually not. Accepting that the very process of running a business brings about a great deal of stress with it means that you have the power to understand and accept that not everything is going to work in your favor every time. There are going to be unexpected difficulties, things are going to go wrong, people are not going to fulfill their expected roles, and other inconveniences are going to arise. This is a simple truth when it comes to running a business. It also happens to be a simple truth in life. Regardless of how badly we want to have completely stress-free lives, it simply is not a possibility. Accepting that stress is a natural and inevitable experience is the first step in reducing how stressful it is when these situations arise. The idea is that if you can accept that they naturally occur, then you are much less likely to feel as though you have any way to control or completely prevent stressful situations from occurring.

When you relinquish this sense of control, you take yourself out of a victim state of mind when stress arises, and you put yourself into a leadership role. Since you are no longer feeling shocked, and overwhelmed when these inevitable stresses arise, you can immediately hop into action and start working to overcome these situations instead.

Reframing your awareness is another great way to reduce the stress you feel. When we are stressed, we often stay entirely focused on everything that is going wrong. Suddenly, just because our delivery was delivered late or something important was missing, we also notice that the stapler has been misplaced, the coffee you ordered was wrong, and someone failed to complete a task on time, therefore, meaning more work for you to endure. When one particularly stressful situation happens, we tend to find stress in many additional areas. However, when we can focus on what is going right and all of the positive aspects of our day and our situation, we can shift our focus back to what is working in our favor. Then, from this positive state of mind, we can easily find solutions for the problems we are being faced with.

Prioritizing is another highly important stress-management task that every person who runs a business needs to master. The larger your business grows, the more in-demand you are going to be. Before you know it, it seems like your to-do list is a mile long, and you are struggling to keep up with it. The more you knock off the list, the more things you have to accomplish to continue moving forward. When you fail to prioritize effectively, everything you set on your list seems equally important. A great way to practice stress-management and time-management simultaneously is to rank your to-do list by two things: due date, and priority level. Then, organize everything on your schedule accordingly. Ensure everything is done on time, in order of what is most important to what is least important. The better you focus on prioritizing and managing your time effectively, the easier it will be for you to reduce the amount of stress you feel from the pressure of your to-do list.

When you are in charge, there tends to be a lot of information that comes flying your way. In an attempt to refrain from forgetting anything important, your brain often holds on to everything. Or at least, it tries to. A great way to reduce the amount of unimportant information floating around in your brain is to practice journaling. You can also use a scheduler. By writing down information, schedules, and important notes right away, you eliminate the need for you to remember them. Then, because your brain doesn't feel the need to retain the information, you can freely let go of it and focus on what is more important. Having too much unimportant information taking up space in your brain can make it harder for you to focus on what is important. It can also make you feel more stressed because the "noise" you have in your brain seems to get louder when there is too much going on in there.

Another way that you can reduce your stress, eliminate free-floating information, and relax is to take frequent breaks. Meditating is a great way to eliminate this extra information, but any form of relaxing will help. Even just taking five minutes to step away from your work and change your scenery can help you when it comes to relaxing and getting your mind clear. While too many breaks can cause you to get distracted and keep you from focusing on your work and being productive, taking regular breaks can ensure that you don't become overwhelmed which can also cause you to struggle to stay focused.

Regular breaks, relaxing, prioritizing, time-management, and reframing your difficult situations are all great strategies of practicing self-care, which is a vital tool when it comes to stress management. If you want to be highly effective at managing your stress, the last thing you want to ensure that you are truly focusing on is self-care. Take the time on a regular basis to ensure that your needs are being met. Go to the bathroom when you need to, drink water, eat well, and ensure that you are giving yourself adequate time to have a personal life and enjoy it as well. Focusing on self-care means that you will be able to reduce your stress, do your best work, and run your business effectively and with great success.

Chapter 4: Productivity

Learning to be productive as a business leader is extremely important. If you run your business alone, you are the only one responsible for getting things done. Therefore, you need to ensure that you are being highly productive so that tasks are being accomplished effectively. If you run a business with employees, you need to be a positive role model to your employees by showing them the art of productivity.

Being a productive leader means that you set the pace for your entire business to run. The more productive you are, the more efficient people are going to be when they are working for you or with you. You will easily accomplish tasks you set on your to-do list, it becomes easier for you to overcome difficulties you may face along the way, and you will find that success is easier to come by as well. People who are productive have significantly higher success rates in their businesses because they are actively accomplishing important tasks that keep their businesses growing and moving forward.

Set Goals

One great way to work toward staying productive is to set goals for yourself. By setting goals, it becomes easier to stay productive. Knowing what you need to achieve to move forward means that you clearly know what action you need to be taking at all times. Often, goals are built in the form of to-do lists. However, when you are running a business you also want to take the time to identify larger goals, beyond what is simply placed on your to-do list. Your larger goals should be the things that you are regularly working toward on a daily basis. You want to use these goals to help you populate your to-do list, ensuring that everything you set out to do will be pushing you toward effectively accomplishing your goals.

A great way to set goals that will help you stay productive in business is to start right away. Begin by taking a "master list" and writing down your biggest business goals. Then, write down smaller goals that you need to take to get toward those larger goals. For example, maybe your goal is to increase your sales volumes to $100,000 each year. You know that to do that, you need more customers. To attract more customers, you need a better marketing system.

Therefore, the first thing you need to be working toward is building better marketing strategies. Then, you can increase your customer list. As your customer list increases, your sales volumes will increase. You can continue expanding on each of these practices until your sales reach your goal amount of $100,000. By having your goals set up and breaking them down in this way, it becomes a lot easier for you to ensure that every single task you are taking is either mandatory for the maintenance of your business, or actively working toward achieving your goals.

When we don't set goals in our businesses, we tend to populate our to-do lists with meaningless tasks that don't actually take us anywhere. Then, even though we are doing a lot, we don't often see results since we are not actually accomplishing any tasks that are results-oriented. To avoid yourself from either feeling lost with nothing to do, or doing plenty but never having any results, you want to ensure that you regularly set goals and work toward them on a daily basis.

Eliminate Distractions

Distractions tend to be a major productivity-killer. As hard as we may try to stay focused, if we are surrounded with too many distractions, we will find that it becomes a lot harder to work. Your phone may notify you about something, and you feel compelled to check the notification. Perhaps your computer internet program has several tabs open, and you remember you were looking at the shopping selection for an online store, so you start shopping again. Then, you realize your printer is out of paper, so you go add more. None of these tasks are likely to be productive to what you were actively trying to do, but because they all stole your attention, they become incredibly important to you all of a sudden. A great way to stay focused is to eliminate distractions. When you are focused, you are productive.

To effectively eliminate distractions, start by looking in your environment. If you notice your overall environment has several distractions in it, begin by taking those away. Although your work environment does not need to be completely bare and can definitely contain inspirational pieces and things that are essential to your productivity, such as office supplies, you do not want to have unnecessary distractions. Anything that may steal away your attention, such as extra pieces of technology, games, or anything else can all be considered distractions. Eliminate these, or at least place them somewhere that is out of sight. Keep your environment clean and clutter-free. To ensure that you are not distracted by anything such as having to refill your printer with paper, have a routine where you come in each morning and check on all of your supplies to make sure that they are filled, fresh, and ready to be used. Then, go ahead and start your day. At the end of each day, clean up your space, so it is ready for the next day.

Aside from your environment, you may also be the cause of your own distractions. Perhaps you choose to bring your phone into your office, and you leave the volume on or the vibration setting on, or maybe you have several games on your phone that you like to play and are easy for you to access. Perhaps, it has nothing to do with any of your physical belongings, but rather your mind. Because you are so distracted by your thoughts, you struggle to stay focused on anything that you are actively trying to accomplish.

First, you want to make sure that you are taking away easy distractions. Practice self-discipline by setting a rule for yourself that you will not be checking anything and will be focusing only on your work for a set amount of time. Then, when that time has passed, go ahead and check your notifications or play your games for a few minutes. If you find that the distractions are because you are thinking about too much, try taking up something such as journaling. Writing everything you are actively thinking about down in your journal is a great way to get it out of your head so that you can return your focus to the task at hand and stay focused.

Delegate Tasks

Delegation is powerful, and it is used in many ways. Parents delegate household chores to children, bosses delegate tasks to employees, humans delegate tasks to animals, there are many times and places where delegation is used to help make completing tasks easier. If you find that you have a lot of work to get done, delegation is a great way to ensure that the tasks are completed on time and with adequate attention to their detail.

In business, there are many things that you can delegate. Even if you cannot to afford regular employees, you can delegate through contractual work. As we discussed in a previous chapter, there are many tasks you can delegate. Hiring an accountant, a virtual assistant, a web designer, and many other types of freelancers are all a great way to help you delegate tasks without having to go through the process of hiring employees.

When it comes to productivity, delegating means that everything can be paid attention to in great detail. Instead of one person struggling to give everything their best attention and efforts, things can be done with the highest level of quality possible. So, even though you may feel like delegating is not the best idea, especially since you will likely have to pay the people you are delegating to, in the long-run it can save money by you having higher quality results to then share with your clients.

Regularly Assess Your Results

The best way to know if you are actually making progress or not is to regularly assess your results. Your results can teach you a lot about your productivity, including where you presently see great results and where you need to improve your practices. Many businesses have a set time for when they will assess their results to see how they are doing. These times are often set out to be quarterly, as this gives them results that have plenty information to read from, meaning their results will be more accurate. Another reason why you want to do your results quarterly is that this means you get to review your efforts multiple times each year, ensuring that you are working toward your goals all year long.

When you are reviewing your results for productivity, you ultimately want to look at each area of your business and see where you are succeeding and where you are struggling. Although you may be inclined to immediately brush off the areas you are succeeding with and focus all of your attention to where you are struggling, this is not ideal. Instead, you want to take a look at your successes and your struggles to give you full insight as to how these results are being produced. For example, say you lead a big team. If you find that your shipping and handling department is working incredibly well and you are having great success there, but your customer service department is struggling to produce positive results, you know that there is a very clear difference taking place between those two departments. One, for example, may have better systems in place, better resources to fulfill their job, more training available for them, or any other number of benefits helping them achieve these results. The other department, namely the one that is struggling, would likely find that they are not gaining all of these benefits and therefore they are struggling. The best thing you can do in this case is to see where the differences lie. Then, with your knowledge, you can enforce changes that will help the struggling department catch up with the successful one.

If you are not running a business filled with employees, you are going to want to look at what you do have. Say you are a running a sole proprietorship and you are the only employee, for example. If you find that you have great success with marketing but that you are struggling with converting sales, you need to address this situation. Perhaps you need to educate yourself more on the sales process, delegate more time to commit to sales, or even hire someone who can help you when it comes to conducting sales calls. There may be many reasons why you succeed more in some areas over others. Perhaps you are more experienced, have a higher level of interested, or simply have more time or better resources to handle certain parts of your business over others. Regardless of what specific cause it is that you are noticing is holding you back, it is important that you recognize this and employ new methods to help you generate success.

Finally, you may still be wondering why it is so important for you to look at the areas that you are succeeding in. Of course, this is a beneficial task if you want to compare these to your less successful areas and discover new methods to succeed. However, there is an additional reason as to why it is crucial that you pay attention to your success as well as your struggles. That is, you want to make sure that you don't stop doing what it is that is making you successful! Just like recognizing these comparisons will help you do better in the areas that you are struggling with, they will also ensure that you keep doing good in the areas that you are having success with. You do not want to mistakenly stop doing something that is bringing you great success because you didn't take the time to identify what that strategy was!

Use A Routine

Finally, routines are a great way to help when it comes to generating productivity. There are several reasons why routines are important, but here are some of the biggest reasons:

- Effective use of time management
- Nothing is forgotten/overlooked
- Easier to focus on each task
- Easy to recognize if there is too much on your plate and you need to delegate
- Steady growth equals steady success

Keeping a routine is excellent for helping with so many areas of your business. Something you should know is how your routine needs to be built. You will likely find several blueprints, examples, outlines, and bouts of information online and elsewhere to help you when it comes to building your routine. While many of these resources offer valuable information toward helping you build your routine, many often fail to mention one important element: your routine only matters if it works for you.

Copying someone else's routine and expecting it to work perfectly for you is not necessarily the best idea. Let's say, for example, they like to read in the morning, but you find it to be boring. You would prefer to read in the afternoon, or maybe you prefer listening to audiobooks in your car or at other times during the day. If this is the case, you need to realize that suddenly adding reading into your morning routine when you don't really care about reading in the morning is not going to help you. In fact, it may break your focus and leave you struggling to stay in sync even more because you are trying to do something that you are simply not interested in.

When you are building your routine, there are three things you need to focus on: efficiency, effectiveness, and customizability. You should pick a routine that is going to efficiently get you through all of the tasks that you need and want to accomplish on a daily basis. Ensure that there is plenty of time for you to complete everything that needs to be done without feeling pressured or rushed to get it all finished. While some pressure is good, too much can break your productivity. If you find this is nearly impossible, start delegating tasks! Effectiveness is similar to efficiency but focuses more so on your ability to actually get things done. The tasks you include in your daily routine should contribute to you effectively moving through your day. For example, adding a "refill office supplies" space on your routine each morning is a great way to ensure that when it comes to fulfilling other tasks throughout the day, you are not left wandering around trying to gather all of the supplies needed. Instead, you thought proactively by adding an effectivity-based task to your routine. Finally, your routine needs to be customizable. This means two things: first, you should be able to customize the routine to what you like, what works for you, and what is going to help you out the most. Second is that your routine should be designed so that if anything ever needs to be changed to accommodate for last minute and unexpected things, you can do so. Don't forget, these are inevitable in business, so trying to create a routine that does not leave room for change will actually go against your ability to be productive, not promote it.

Chapter 5: Networking

As someone who runs a business, the power of networking serves you on a variety of levels. There are many ways that people who run businesses are benefitted by the process of networking. We are going to explore these ways in this chapter.

Networking is the act of getting to know new people in your network. Essentially, you are intentionally setting aside time to work toward building relationships with people who are in a similar industry, or who may somehow help you out in the future. While your sole intention does not need to be for personal gain, the idea that you can help each other out is often a very large part of what brings you together with the people in your network.

There are many major ways that people in your network can help you out. You can also help them in many of these ways, which ultimately makes the relationship mutually beneficial. These ways include things such as:

- Client referrals
- Helping with marketing

- Advising new merchants, suppliers, resources, etc.

- Introducing you to new people in your mutual network

- Increase brand visibility and awareness

- Shared knowledge

- New opportunities

- Building confidence

As you can tell, these benefits stand to offer a major positive impact when it comes to running a business. So, if you are not already networking, you definitely need to start! Whether you are or are not already involved in networking, there are many incredible tips you can use to help you when it comes to effectively networking with others in the business. The following tips will provide you with pointers on how you can increase your networking skills and expand your network rapidly, and with quality.

Get Involved

The first step to effectively networking is actually putting yourself out there. By intentionally going out and getting involved in events that will help you network, you infinitely increase your odds of building your network! There are many ways that you can get involved to help you in this situation. To get started online, you can join social media groups that are built around your particular industry. Regularly commenting on various posts and communicating with people in the groups is a great way to get yourself out there and get seen without having to go out of your way much on a day-to-day basis. Otherwise, going out to actual networking events such as charity galas, networking dinners or luncheons, and other networking-oriented events are a great way to get involved and start meeting people who are a part of your community! You can also attend events where people within your network would likely hangout, such as launch parties, industry-specific events such as fashion shows or seminars, and other similar events. By putting yourself out there and strategically placing yourself in areas where people from your network are likely to hang out, you infinitely increase your chances of being seen and building your network.

Nurture the Right Relationships

When it comes to networking, you always want to make sure that you are nurturing the right relationships. Just like you wouldn't want to date someone anymore after knowing that the relationship was not going anywhere, do not pursue networking relationships that do not serve both parties. Of course, this does not mean that you should be mean to or cold-shoulder anyone who you do not see as an immediate benefit to you. Remember, you can always learn from people. As well, you don't want to be seen as someone who might only be using others. The best thing you can do is keep a relationship with everyone, but really focusing on nurturing the ones that have the power to make a difference in your business, and you in theirs.

Join or Start a Networking Group

Many communities have networking groups, and if yours doesn't you can always start one! Networking groups are typically comprised of a selection of people who meet on a regular basis to discuss business, talk about their growth, share knowledge, and make connections. Getting involved in these groups gives you the best opportunity to really boost your network. There are many online sources you can look to that will help you discover a new networking group. However, if you don't find any that you feel fits what you are looking for, you can always start your own! Simply set aside a date and get involved, and before you know it, you will be on your way to building an incredible networking community. If you don't feel that you have the time to do it in person, you can always build an online one that is somewhat self-sufficient, too!

In addition to these strategies, you may also find organic networking opportunities arise. For example, you might meet someone in a grocery store or elsewhere in the community and learn through a random conversation that they are also a part of the same industry as you are. For this reason, never turn yourself away from those around you. Instead, learn to open up conversations with people and learn more about them. In time, you will find that you are rapidly expanding your network and adding new people to it all of the time. If you have interactions that don't pan out, you can always take away the social skills you learned from each interaction so that you can make all future interactions successful and positive! Never look at any conversation or connection as a waste of time or a missed opportunity. Instead, they are all lessons to be learned and potential to expand.

Chapter 6: Self-Awareness

Self-awareness is a vital skill when you are running a business. As a leader, it is crucial that you can keep yourself "in check" if you are ever going to be able to keep everything else in check, too. If you are incapable of determining what you are and aren't capable of, you are going to struggle to manage everything effectively.

Leaders who are self-aware are far more effective and productive when it comes to leading their company, and a team of people. There are many reasons why, which we are going to explore further, now.

Emotional Intelligence

Emotional intelligence is powerful when it comes to leaders. Self-awareness happens to be one of the leading skills in building emotional intelligence. When a leader is emotionally intelligent, it becomes far easier for them to create success in their business. For starters, they are capable of emotionally leading a team. What that means is: rather than them being emotionally distraught and their team following their lead, an emotionally intelligent leader can calm themselves and regulate their emotions effectively. Then, they can also help their team do the same. If you are working independently, being able to regulate your own emotions means that you can effectively stay on-task to complete the many tasks you have left on your to-do list. If you have a team, it means that you can effectively keep everyone on task. You are more effective in calming down upset employees, motivating bored or unfocused employees, and ultimately leading your team on an emotional level. When you can do this, you make it infinitely easier to get yourself and your team working together toward your mutual goals.

Life Management Skills

Some of the skills we have discussed previously in this book include time management, stress management, and self-discipline. Each of these tasks are far easier to actually accomplish when you possess the skill of being self-aware. If you want to become a highly productive and effective leader, becoming self-aware of how you are in various life circumstances means that you can also develop an awareness of how you overcome these various struggles. Then, instead of stressfully scrambling to find a solution when troubles arise, you are already fairly clear on what you need to do to move through almost any situation. If you want to be more effective at leading yourself by becoming more productive, less stressed, and more results-oriented, practice self-awareness. This simple change will make everything significantly easier for you to achieve.

Team Management Skills

Naturally, if you are more effective at leading yourself, you will be more effective at leading a team. By building your self-awareness and working on life management skills that you can use in your business in your own life, you become a positive role model for your team. This means any time that you are actively leading them, they are going to feel motivated to take after you. It will be easier for them to follow your high energy and productive skills if you are demonstrating them each day. Furthermore, by being self-aware, you can also become more aware on how you are leading your team. You will be able to recognize when you may be coming down too harsh on people, expecting too much, or otherwise making their job more stressful by your very presence. If you can become self-aware over these elements, you can also develop a new strategy to help you overcome these tendencies and find new ways to lead your team with a more positive influence.

Building your self-awareness ultimately comes from learning to stop and reflect on how you operate as a leader. Pay attention to how you interact with others, how various situations make you feel, and your general response to these situations. Always take the time to sit back and reflect so that you can look for opportunities to improve your strategies. The easiest way to do this is to schedule time for reflection. However, you can also begin implementing a new strategy where you pause for a few moments after each interaction and challenge and reflect on how it went. Pay attention to how you acted in the situation, including how you helped the situation and how you made it worse. Be extremely honest with yourself, and refrain from placing blame elsewhere. Look only at how you behaved, and what you could have done to increase the success of the situation. If it already was successful, pay attention to what you did to get it there and how you can use these successful skills to help you in future situations that you may find difficult.

The more you can look at yourself and reflect on yourself, the easier it becomes for you to practice self-awareness. Then, you can use your self-awareness to increase your ability to manage yourself and how you run your business, and anyone whom you may have hired or intend to hire in the future.

Chapter 7: Customer Awareness

Running a business is nothing if you don't have customers. After all, businesses don't exist without them! If you want to successfully run a business, you need to develop skills in the customer awareness category. By increasing your awareness of your customers, how your business looks to them, and how you can put them at the center of everything you do, you create a greater chance for you to experience success in growing your business.

Customer awareness is something that many companies talk about but few actually deeply understand. Unfortunately, by not effectively employing this skill, they often leave bad impressions for their customers and actually drive them away rather than attracting them in. To avoid you having any negative experiences with your own customer awareness practices, let's explore some positive customer awareness skills you need to pay attention to.

Listen to What They're Saying

More often than not, your customers will directly tell you what they think of your business. They will provide you with their experiences, often through feedback. It is important to understand that there are only two times that a customer will go out of their way to provide feedback, however. The first is when they absolutely love your company. When they have had an incredible experience and really enjoyed their interaction with your company, they will go out of their way to rave about you. This is ultimately what most businesses strive for. The other time is when they have had an awful experience. When a customer has been severely inconvenienced or wronged by your company, they will go out of their way to tell people about this experience. Listen to what they're saying both times.

From positive experiences, you can learn more about what people are enjoying about your company. If you will recall from what you have learned about productivity, knowing more about what you are doing that is working means that you can keep doing it and continue getting raving reviews for it. It can also give you an idea of how you can adjust other processes so that you generate success there, too.

From negative experiences, you want to do your best to find every possible area where the person experienced trouble. Then, it is crucial that you look for opportunities to fix these troubles both for said person and all future customers. Never shrug at bad feedback, as this feedback has the power to cripple your company. Instead, pay attention to it, take it seriously, and implement all changes necessary. If it tends to be something that many people complain about, you will want to do your best to ensure that you also clearly and publicly state that you are adjusting these systems to ensure that these troubles are dissolved, and no future customers experience them. Of course, take the time to also apologize to the ones who have and to do your best to do right by them so that they may give your company a second chance.

Listen to What They're Not Saying

So, if customers only speak when they extremely like or extremely dislike your company, this means there is a lot that they are not telling you. For that reason, you either need to ask them through quizzes or questionnaires, or look for the things they're not saying. You can listen to what your customers are not saying by analyzing the data of your company. If your sales volumes are increasing and you are maintaining positive non-verbal ratings (e.g., five-star product ratings online) your customers are telling you that they enjoy your company and they are happy with their experience. If you see your sales volumes decline, lower online ratings, less engagement with your marketing strategies, or are otherwise noticing a decline in your success rates, then your customers are telling you they are unhappy. They may be unhappy because they simply did not like or need your products or services, you may be selling stuff that is out of style or not on-trend, or they may have had experiences that were bad enough that they didn't want to come back, but also that they didn't feel the need to complain about it. Either way, you need to look at this as a sign that your customers are unhappy. Depending on your situation, the exact metrics you are holding, and what you have directly heard, you can then adjust your course and rebuild your program to help you revive your success going forward.

Look at Your Business from Their Perspective

It is crucial that you always take the time to pay attention to what your business looks like from the eyes of your customer. Customers want to see a business that is attractive, professional, engaging, and polite. They want you to be trendy, effective, productive, and capable of providing them with positive experiences. When you take the time to regard your business from your customer's perspective, you give yourself the ability to step into their shoes and honestly see how effective (or ineffective) your company is at meeting their needs.

Depending on your business model, there are many ways that you may step into the shoes of your customer. If you are store-based, walk into your store through the front doors and look at your displays. Notice if they are clean and professional, or disorganized or broken. Pay attention to your staff, how you are greeted, and how they treat you. Look at their uniforms, too. You also want to see how effective the sales process is. Is it easy for you to get the help you need and acquire your products or services? Or are there several steps, challenges, and struggles you face along the way? Make sure everything is running smoothly for the customer.

The same goes for an online store or business. Look at your website and analyze how it looks. Is it professional, or does it look like it could use a facelift? Are the features working? Can you easily locate anything you may be looking for? Are the pictures attractive and clean? Do they line up properly? Do the colors match? How easy is it to look at your site? Are there too many decorations, or maybe not enough? Is the font easy to read? Get really critical about this. If you conduct sales through your website, you also want to look at this process and see how easy it is for customers to purchase things through your website. Look at your social media accounts with this type of critical thinking also, to ensure that they are also appealing to your customer and benefitting your business. Your entire online presence should be clean, professional, attractive, approachable, and enjoyable.

Always Focus on Customer Experience

Do not make the mistake of becoming complacent once you have found a system that works. While you don't want to drastically change a perfectly operable system, you also don't want to assume that your existing system will stand the test of time. Continually look for opportunities to make small adjustments to keep the customer experience positive and enjoyable. If you find new technology that could improve the speed or efficiency of a certain task, make use of it! If you find that you have a new way you can display the products that are more attractive and easy to navigate, try it out! You can always change back to the old system if the new one doesn't work. However, it is much harder to revive your reputation after you have been deemed "outdated," "difficult to use," or otherwise inconvenient for customers.

Conclusion

Congratulations on reading *"How to Direct a Business: 7 Skills You Must Develop to Succeed"*!

Running a business is no easy feat, but with these seven skills, you can develop your business effortlessly! Whether you have an existing business, or you are brand new in the business world, these seven steps can help you scale your business and experience great success in it.

I hope that these steps were able to provide you with great insight on how you can start running your business more effectively and growing it more efficiently, regardless of where you are already at. Whether you have a significant amount of finances or only a few to invest, these skills will help you get to where you want to be. You can start with zero customers, a hundred, or even a hundred thousand and these skills will still help you improve your systems and run a business with greater strength than ever before.

The next step is to work toward building these skills regularly. Revisit your systems, implement these seven steps, and practice them on a regular basis. Do not allow yourself to become complacent, especially once you begin seeing results. Instead, continue practicing these skills so that you can develop them with greater efficiency and experience great success as a result.

Lastly, if you enjoyed this book, I ask that you, please take the time to review it on Amazon Kindle honestly. Your feedback would be greatly appreciated!

Thank you

Book Description

Running a business is not always easy, but these seven steps can help make it a breeze. By effectively using the seven steps that you will find in "How to Direct a Business: 7 Skills You Must Develop to Succeed", you can greatly increase your chances of having success in your business.

There are many skills required when it comes to running a business. These skills go beyond the actual working processes of the business and expand into important subjects like self-discipline, stress-management, and customer awareness. When you take the time to develop these skills, you significantly improve your leadership abilities. As a great leader, it becomes almost inevitable that you will experience massive success in your business.

If you are ready to learn how you can develop the seven most important skills that every business owner and operator needs to succeed, this book is perfect for you. You will learn about these skills in-depth so that you can begin implementing them immediately. These tips can be applied immediately, regardless of whether you are brand new with zero customers and revenue, or if you have been in business for some time already and have successfully generated revenue and customers. Expanding on these seven skills will ensure that you create a system that works so efficiently that your growth is massive and launches your business into a total success.

If this is what you are looking for, then look no further! Download *"How to Direct a Business: 7* Skills You Must Develop to Succeed" today and get yourself to the top, now!